Wealth Building 101: Expert Tips and Actionable Advice"

JOHNSON RYAN

TABLE OF CONTENTS

Chapter ONE INTRODUCTION TO WEALTH BUILDING 101

Welcome to Wealth Building 101, where we unravel the principles, **expert tips**, and **actionable advice** essential for cultivating financial prosperity.

: In this guide, we'll explore key strategies that empower individuals to build and grow their wealth over time.
: From smart saving and investing to strategic financial planning, let's delve into the foundational elements that pave the way to long-term financial success.
: Whether you're just starting your wealth-building journey or looking to optimize your current approach, these insights will serve as a comprehensive roadmap to guide you towards a more secure and prosperous future.

Overview of Wealth Building

Wealth Structure 101" is a comprehensive companion immolation **expert tips** and practicable advice for fiscal substance. It covers abecedarian principles, similar as budgeting, saving, and investing. The companion emphasizes the significance of setting clear fiscal pretensions, creating a realistic budget, and constantly saving a portion of income. It delves into colorful investment strategies, from stocks and real estate to diversifying portfolios for long- term growth. also, it provides perceptivity on debt operation, emphasizing the significance of reducing high-interest debts. Overall," **Wealth Building** aims to empower individualities with practical tools and knowledge to secure their fiscal future.

Wealth structure goes beyond the basics, probing into the nuances of fiscal success. It stresses the significance of understanding the power of emulsion interest and encourages individualities to start investing beforehand for maximum impact. The companion also covers threat operation, educating compendiums on how to assess their threat forbearance and choose investments aligned with their fiscal pretensions.

likewise, it explores the part of unresistant income aqueducts, similar as tips or rental income, in erecting wealth. The companion highlights the significance of staying informed about request trends and conforming strategies consequently. It also addresses the cerebral aspect of plutocrat operation, emphasizing discipline, tolerance, and the capability to ride request oscillations.

Also," .." advocates for nonstop literacy, suggesting coffers and tools to stay streamlined on fiscal trends and investment openings. It serves as a roadmap, guiding compendiums through colorful life stages and helping them acclimate their wealth- structure strategies consequently.

In substance, the companion provides a holistic approach to wealth structure, combining practical fiscal advice with a mindset shift towards long- term fiscal success.

Importance Of Financial Literacy

Financial literacy is crucial for wealth building as it empowers individuals to make informed and strategic decisions about their finances. Understanding concepts like budgeting, investing, and debt management enables people to optimize their financial resources. With knowledge of basic financial principles, individuals can create effective plans for saving and investing, ultimately leading to the growth of their wealth over time.

Expert Tip 1: Budgeting Mastery : Create a detailed budget to track income and expenses.Allocate funds strategically, prioritizing savings and investments.Regularly review and adjust the budget based on changing financial circumstances.

Expert Tip 2: Debt Management : Understand the types of debt and prioritize paying off high-interest debts.Avoid accumulating unnecessary debt and utilize credit wisely.Establish a plan to systematically reduce and eliminate outstanding debts.

Expert Tip 3: Investing Knowledge : Learn about various investment options, such as stocks, bonds, and real estate.Diversify investments to manage risk effectively.Stay informed about market trends and adjust investment strategies accordingly.

Expert Tip 4: Emergency Fund : Essentials Build and maintain an emergency fund for unexpected expenses.Aim for three to six months' worth of living expenses in the emergency fund.This fund provides a financial safety net, preventing the need to dip into investments during emergencies.

Expert Tip 5: Retirement Planning : Understand retirement savings vehicles like 401(k)s and IRAs.Start saving for retirement early to benefit from compounding growth.Continuously reassess retirement goals and adjust contributions accordingly.

Expert Tip 6: Continuous Learning : Stay informed about financial trends, economic changes, and new investment opportunities.Attend financial literacy workshops, read books, and follow reputable financial news sources.Adapt and refine financial strategies based on ongoing learning.

In conclusion, financial literacy serves as the cornerstone of wealth building. It empowers individuals to navigate the complexities of personal finance, make informed decisions, and ultimately achieve long-term financial success. By implementing expert tips and actionable advice, individuals can proactively manage their finances, build wealth, and secure a more financially stable future.

Chapter TWO SETTING FINANCIAL GOALS

Setting financial goals is a crucial step in the wealth-building journey. Here's a breakdown of the process:

1. **Define Clear Objectives**:Clearly articulate your financial objectives, such as buying a home, saving for education, or retirement.Specify the amount needed and the timeline for each goal.

2. **Prioritize Goals**:Prioritize your goals based on urgency and importance.Distinguish between short-term goals (1-3 years), medium-term goals (4-10 years), and long-term goals (10+ years).

3. **Quantify Your Goals**:Assign a specific monetary value to each goal.This helps in creating a realistic and achievable savings plan.

4. **Create a Budget**:Analyze your current income and expenses to understand your financial position.Allocate a portion of your income towards savings and investments.

5. **Emergency Fund**:Prioritize building an emergency fund equivalent to 3-6 months of living expenses.This provides a financial cushion in case of unexpected events.

6. **Debt Management**:Identify and prioritize high-interest debts for repayment.Develop a strategy to gradually eliminate outstanding debts.

7. **Investment Strategy**:Diversify investments to manage risk.Consider a mix of stocks, bonds, real estate, and other investment vehicles based on your risk tolerance and time horizon.

8. **Regular Review**:Periodically assess your financial goals and adjust them based on changing circumstances.Modify your budget and investment strategy accordingly.

9. **Automate Savings**:Set up automatic transfers to your savings and investment accounts.This ensures consistency and discipline in building wealth.

10. **Educate Yourself**:Stay informed about investment options, market trends, and financial planning strategies.Continuous learning empowers you to make informed decisions.

11. **Seek Professional Advice**:Consult with financial advisors for personalized guidance.Professionals can help tailor strategies to your unique financial situation.

12. **Celebrate Milestones:**Acknowledge and celebrate achievements along the way.This positive reinforcement encourages continued financial discipline.

By following these steps, you can lay a solid foundation for wealth building, fostering financial security and achieving your long-term objectives.

Short-term vs. Long-term Goals

Short-Term Goals:

1) **Definition:**
   Short-term goals typically span 1-3 years.
   Examples include building an emergency fund, saving for a vacation, or paying off high-interest debt.

2) **Actionable Advice:**Prioritize immediate needs and high-interest debt repayment.Focus on liquid and low-risk investments, like savings accounts or short-term bonds.

3) **Flexibility:**Short-term goals offer flexibility for adjustments.Reassess and modify these goals as circumstances change.

4) **Emergency Fund:**Establishing a robust emergency fund is a primary short-term goal.This fund provides a financial safety net for unexpected expenses.

5) **Budgeting:**Create a detailed budget to allocate funds towards short-term objectives.Regularly track and adjust spending to meet these goals.

Long-Term Goals:

1. **Definition:**Long-term goals extend beyond 10 years and often involve significant financial milestones like retirement or purchasing a home.

2. **Actionable Advice:**Emphasize growth-oriented investments, such as a diversified portfolio of stocks and real estate.Leverage the power of compounding by starting early and staying invested.

3. **Risk Tolerance**:Long-term goals allow for a higher risk tolerance.Volatility in the market has more time to average out over the long term.

4. **Retirement Planning:**Saving for retirement is a key long-term goal.Take advantage of retirement accounts like 401(k)s and IRAs to maximize tax benefits.

5. **Education and Skill Development**:Long-term wealth building may involve investing in education or skills.Continuously enhancing your abilities can contribute to increased earning potential.

6. **Review and Adjust:**Regularly review and adjust your long-term goals.Factors like career changes, economic conditions, or personal circumstances may necessitate modifications.

7. **Estate Planning**:Include estate planning as part of long-term goals.Ensure that your wealth is distributed according to your wishes by creating a will and considering trusts.

8. **Consistency:**Consistency is key in long-term wealth building.Stick to your investment and savings strategy even during market fluctuations.

9. **Balancing Short-Term and Long-Term Goals**:Prioritization:Balance short-term needs with long-term objectives.Ensure that meeting immediate financial obligations doesn't hinder progress towards future goals.

10. **Emergency Fund Maintenance**:Even as you focus on long-term goals, continue to maintain and replenish your emergency fund for unforeseen expenses.

11. **Regular Review:**Periodically review and adjust both short-term and long-term goals.This ensures alignment with your evolving financial situation and objectives.

By understanding and effectively balancing short-term and long-term goals, you can build a comprehensive wealth-building strategy that addresses immediate needs while laying the groundwork for sustained financial services.

Smart Goal Setting

1. **Specific (S):** Clearly define your financial objectives. For instance, specify the amount of wealth you aim to accumulate, whether through savings, investments, or other means.

2. **Measurable (M):** Establish tangible criteria to track progress. Instead of a vague goal like "increase wealth," set a measurable target such as "achieve a 10% annual increase in savings and investments."

3. **Achievable (A):** Ensure your goals are realistic and attainable within your current financial situation. Avoid setting overly ambitious targets that may lead to frustration or financial strain.
4. **Relevant (R):** Align your wealth-building goals with your broader financial objectives and life aspirations. Consider whether each goal contributes meaningfully to your overall financial well-being.

5. **Time-Bound (T):** Set specific timeframes for achieving your goals. For example, plan to save a certain amount within a year or reach a specific investment milestone within five years. This adds urgency and structure to your wealth-building plan.

Expert Tips:

6. **Diversify Investments**: Spread your investments across various asset classes to mitigate risk and maximize potential returns. This could include stocks, bonds, real estate, and other financial instruments.

7. **Emergency Fund**: Prioritize building an emergency fund to cover unexpected expenses. This ensures financial stability and prevents setbacks to your wealth-building journey.

8. **Continuous Learning:** Stay informed about personal finance and investment strategies. Regularly update your knowledge to make informed decisions in a dynamic financial landscape.

9. **Budgeting**: Create a detailed budget to manage expenses effectively. Track spending habits and identify areas where you can cut back to allocate more funds towards wealth-building activities.

10. **Professional Advice**: Consult with financial advisors or experts to tailor your wealth-building strategy to your unique circumstances. They can provide personalized insights and guide you through complex financial decisions.

Actionable Advice:

11. **Set Monthly Savings Targets**: Determine a specific amount to save each month. Automate transfers to your savings or investment accounts to ensure consistency.

12. **Debt Reduction Plan:** Develop a plan to systematically pay down high-interest debts. This frees up more resources for wealth-building activities.

13. **Regular Financial Checkups**: Schedule regular reviews of your financial goals and progress. Adjust your strategies as needed to adapt to changing circumstances.

14. **Side Income Streams:** Explore opportunities for additional income, such as freelance work, investments, or a side business. This extra income can accelerate wealth accumulation.

15. **Periodic Reassessment**: Periodically reassess your goals and adjust them based on changing priorities, financial circumstances, and market conditions.

By combining SMART goal-setting principles with expert tips and actionable advice, you can create a robust and adaptable wealth-building plan tailored to your financial aspirations.

Chapter THREE BUDGETING BASICS

Budgeting is a fundamental aspect of wealth building, serving as a strategic roadmap to financial success. Here's a breakdown of key principles and actionable advice:

1. **Income Assessment:**Understand your monthly income from all sources.Differentiate between fixed (salary) and variable (bonuses, side income) earnings.

2. **Expense Tracking:**Categorize your spending (e.g., housing, groceries, entertainment).Utilize budgeting apps to monitor expenses in real-time.

3. **Emergency Fund:**Prioritize building an emergency fund to cover 3-6 months of living expenses.Safeguard against unforeseen financial challenges.

4. **Debt Management:**Identify and prioritize high-interest debts for repayment.Allocate a portion of your budget to debt reduction each month.

5. **Savings Goals:**Establish short-term and long-term savings goals (e.g., vacations, retirement).Automate savings contributions to ensure consistency.

6. **Investment Strategy:**Diversify investments to mitigate risk.Regularly review and adjust your investment portfolio based on financial goals and market conditions.

7. **Live Below Your Means:**Differentiate between needs and wants.Cultivate a mindset of frugality to save more for future wealth creation.

8. **Continuous Education:**Stay informed about personal finance and investment opportunities.Attend workshops, read books, and follow reputable financial experts for insights.

9. **Review and Adjust:**Regularly reassess your budget to accommodate changing circumstances.Adjust allocations based on evolving priorities and financial goals.

10. **Tax Planning:**Understand tax implications of your income and investments.Leverage tax-efficient strategies to optimize returns.

11. **Automate Finances**:Set up automatic bill payments and savings transfers.Streamline financial processes to reduce the risk of oversights.

12. **Mindful Spending**:Practice conscious spending by aligning purchases with your values and goals.Avoid impulsive buys and assess the long-term impact of financial decisions.

Remember, building wealth is a gradual process, and consistent adherence to a well-structured budget lays the foundation for financial prosperity. Adjustments and continuous learning are essential components of this journey.

Creating a Personal Budget

Creating a personal budget is a crucial step in wealth building, providing a clear framework for managing finances effectively. Here's a comprehensive guide with expert tips and actionable advice:

1. **Assess Your Financial Situation:**Begin by understanding your current financial standing, including income, expenses, assets, and debts.

2. **Set Clear Financial Goals:**Define short-term and long-term financial goals, such as saving for an emergency fund, paying off debts, or investing for retirement.

3. **Categorize Your Expenses:**Identify and categorize your spending into fixed (e.g., rent, utilities) and variable (e.g., dining out, entertainment) expenses.

4. **Determine Your Income:**Calculate your total monthly income, including salary, bonuses, and any additional income streams.

5. **Emergency Fund Allocation:**Prioritize allocating a portion of your income towards building and maintaining an emergency fund. This serves as a financial safety net.
6. **Debt Repayment Strategy:**Allocate a specific amount to repay high-interest debts. Prioritize debts with the highest interest rates to save on interest payments.

7. **Savings Allocation:**Allocate a percentage of your income to savings. This can include contributions to retirement accounts, investment accounts, and other savings goals.

8. **Budgeting Apps and Tools:**Utilize budgeting apps and tools to streamline the budgeting process. These tools can help track expenses, set spending limits, and provide insights into your financial habits.

9. **Live Below Your Means**:Adopt a lifestyle that allows you to spend less than you earn. Differentiate between essential needs and discretionary spending.

10. **Regularly Review Your Budget**:Schedule regular reviews to assess your budget's effectiveness. Adjust allocations based on changes in income, expenses, or financial goals.

11. **Automate Savings and Payments**:Set up automated transfers for savings and bill payments. Automation ensures consistency and minimizes the risk of missed payments.

12. **Prioritize Investments**:Allocate funds for investments based on your risk tolerance and financial goals. Diversify your investment portfolio for long-term wealth growth.

13. **Tax-Efficient Planning**:Be aware of tax implications and leverage tax-efficient strategies to maximize your income and investments.Emergency Fund Maintenance:Regularly assess and replenish your emergency fund, especially after unexpected expenses or changes in income.

14. **Educate Yourself Continuously**:Stay informed about personal finance trends, investment opportunities, and financial planning strategies. Knowledge is key to making informed financial decisions.

Creating and adhering to a personal budget is a cornerstone of wealth building. It empowers you to take control of your financial future, make intentional choices, and work towards achieving your financial aspirations.

Tracking Expenses

Tracking expenses is a fundamental aspect of wealth building. By meticulously monitoring your spending, you gain valuable insights into your financial habits. Here's a breakdown of expert tips and actionable advice for effective expense tracking on your wealth-building journey:

1. **Create a Detailed Budget:**Start by outlining your monthly income and fixed expenses.Categorize discretionary spending areas like entertainment, dining out, and shopping.

2. **Use Technology to Your Advantage:**Leverage budgeting apps and tools to automate expense tracking.Set up alerts to stay informed about overspending in specific categories.

3. **Regularly Review and Adjust:**Schedule periodic reviews of your budget to ensure accuracy.Adjust spending categories based on changing priorities or financial goals.

4. **Emergency Fund Allocation:**Allocate a portion of your income to an emergency fund for unexpected expenses.This safeguards your long-term investments from being disrupted by unforeseen financial setbacks.

5. **Prioritize High-Impact Spending:**Identify and prioritize expenses that contribute significantly to your goals.Cut back on low-impact spending to allocate more resources to wealth-building activities.

6. **Monitor and Negotiate Bills:**Regularly check utility bills, insurance premiums, and subscriptions.Negotiate better deals and consider switching providers to reduce fixed expenses.

7. **Debt Reduction Strategy**:Develop a plan to systematically reduce and eliminate high-interest debts.Allocate extra funds to paying off debts to free up more money for wealth-building endeavors.

8. **Invest Surplus Wisely**:Invest any surplus funds in diversified, long-term assets like stocks or real estate.Reinvest dividends and returns to accelerate wealth accumulation.

9. **Educate Yourself Continuously**:Stay informed about personal finance and investment strategies.Attend workshops, read books, or follow financial experts to refine your wealth-building knowledge.

10. **Celebrate Milestones and Adjust Goals**:Acknowledge and celebrate financial milestones.Periodically reassess your goals, adjusting them based on evolving life circumstances.

Remember, successful wealth building involves a combination of disciplined expense tracking, strategic investments, and continuous learning. By implementing these tips, you lay a strong foundation for achieving long-term financial success.

Chapter FOUR Saving Strategies

Saving is a crucial component of wealth building, providing the foundation for future investments and financial security. Here are expert tips and actionable advice to optimize your saving strategies in Wealth Building 101:

1) **Establish Clear Goals**:Define specific short-term and long-term financial goals.Having a clear purpose for saving helps you stay motivated and focused.Automate Savings:Set up automatic transfers to a dedicated savings account.Automation ensures consistent contributions without relying on manual effort.

2) **Emergency Fund Priority**:Prioritize building an emergency fund to cover 3-6 months of living expenses.This safeguards against unforeseen financial challenges and prevents the need to dip into investments.

3) **Pay Yourself First**:Allocate a portion of your income to savings before covering other expenses.Treat saving as a non-negotiable expense to prioritize your financial future.

4) **Cut Unnecessary Expenses**:Identify and eliminate non-essential spending to free up more funds for saving.Evaluate monthly subscriptions, dining out, and impulse purchases.

5) **Create a Spending Plan:**Develop a detailed budget that clearly outlines income, expenses, and savings goals.Regularly review and adjust the plan to accommodate changing financial circumstances.

6) **Take Advantage of Employer Benefits**:Contribute to employer-sponsored retirement plans, such as 401(k) or pension programs.Maximize employer matching contributions to enhance your savings.

7) **Explore Tax-Advantaged Accounts**:Utilize tax-advantaged accounts like IRAs or HSAs to optimize savings.Understand the tax implications of your investment choices to maximize returns.

8) **Diversify Savings Vehicles**:Explore different savings instruments, including high-yield savings accounts, CDs, and investment accounts.Diversification helps balance risk and return in your savings portfolio.

9) **Review and Increase Contributions**:Regularly review your savings contributions and make adjustments as your income grows.Gradually increase the percentage of your income dedicated to savings over time.

10) **Avoid Lifestyle Inflation**:Resist the temptation to increase spending significantly with salary raises.Redirect additional income towards savings to accelerate wealth accumulation.

11) **Educate Yourself on Investments**:Learn about various investment options to make informed decisions.Understand the risk-return profile of investments and align them with your financial goals.

By incorporating these saving strategies into your wealth-building plan, you can establish a solid financial foundation and pave the way for sustained growth and prosperity.

Emergency Fund Essentials

Building and maintaining an emergency fund is a critical aspect of financial planning and wealth building. Here are expert tips and actionable advice on essential elements for an effective emergency fund in Wealth Building 101:

1. **Set a Target Amount:**Determine a target for your emergency fund, typically 3 to 6 months' worth of living expenses.Consider individual circumstances such as job stability and family size when setting the amount.

2. **Prioritize Liquidity:**Keep the emergency fund in highly liquid and easily accessible accounts.Opt for savings accounts or money market accounts to ensure quick access in times of need.

3. **Separate from Regular Accounts:**Maintain a separate account specifically designated for the emergency fund.This separation helps prevent unintentional spending and ensures the fund is preserved for its intended purpose.

4. **Regularly Contribute:**Consistently contribute to the emergency fund, even if in small amounts.Set up automatic transfers to ensure a disciplined approach to building the fund over time.

5. **Reassess and Adjust:**Periodically reassess your living expenses and adjust the fund amount accordingly.Life changes, such as a new job or family additions, may necessitate an increase in the emergency fund.Use Windfalls Wisely:Allocate unexpected windfalls, like tax refunds or bonuses, to bolster the emergency fund.This accelerates fund growth without impacting your regular budget.

6. **Cover Various Scenarios:**Consider potential emergencies such as medical expenses, car repairs, or job loss when determining fund size.The fund should provide a financial safety net for a range of unforeseen circumstances.

7. **Avoid Investment Risks:**Keep the emergency fund separate from investment portfolios.While it's essential to grow wealth through investments, the emergency fund's primary purpose is immediate access to cash in emergencies.

8. **Replenish Promptly:**If you need to use the emergency fund, replenish it as soon as possible.Maintaining the fund's intended level ensures ongoing financial protection.

9. **Review Insurance Coverage:**Ensure you have adequate insurance coverage for health, property, and other critical areas.This reduces reliance on the emergency fund for certain types of unexpected expenses.

10. **Educate Family Members:**Communicate the purpose of the emergency fund to family members.Having a shared understanding encourages responsible financial behavior within the household.

11. **Adapt to Life Changes:**As life circumstances change, such as marriage or the birth of a child, revisit and adjust the emergency fund.Adapting to changing needs ensures the fund remains relevant and effective.

By incorporating these essentials into your emergency fund strategy, you fortify your financial resilience, allowing you to navigate unexpected challenges without compromising your long-term wealth-building goals.

Benefits of Automated Savings

Automated savings play a pivotal role in wealth building by introducing efficiency, consistency, and discipline into your financial habits. Here are the benefits of automated savings, along with expert tips and actionable advice in Wealth Building 101:

1. **Consistency and Discipline**:
   Benefit: Automation ensures regular contributions to savings without relying on manual efforts.
   Tip: Set up automated transfers to your savings account on payday to establish a consistent saving routine.

2. **Reduced Procrastination**:
   Benefit: Automation eliminates the tendency to procrastinate or forget to save.
   Tip: Schedule automated transfers immediately after receiving your paycheck to prioritize savings.

3. **Stress-Free Financial Management**:
   Benefit: Automating savings simplifies financial management, reducing stress and cognitive load.Tip: Use budgeting apps that offer automated savings features to streamline the process.

4. **Accelerated Goal Achievement**:
   Benefit: Automated contributions help you reach savings goals faster.
   Tip: Increase automated transfers when you receive a salary raise or additional income.

5. **Emergency Fund Building**:
   Benefit: Consistent automated contributions efficiently build and maintain an emergency fund.
   Tip: Allocate a fixed percentage of your income to automatically go into your emergency fund.

6. **Harnessing the Power of Compounding**:
   Benefit: Automated investing leverages the compounding effect over time.

Tip: Set up automated contributions to investment accounts to maximize long-term growth potential.

7. **Avoiding Lifestyle Inflation**:
   Benefit: Automation helps prevent spending increases with income growth.
   Tip: Direct a portion of salary raises or windfalls automatically into savings to counteract lifestyle inflation.

8. **Timely Bill Payments**:
   Benefit: Automating bill payments ensures timely settlements, avoiding late fees.
   Tip: Use auto-pay features for recurring bills to maintain financial discipline.

9. **Customizable Automation:**
   Benefit: Automation can be tailored to suit individual financial goals and needs.
   Tip: Explore options to automate various savings goals, such as retirement, education, or a home purchase.

10. **Improved Financial Health**:
    Benefit: Regular, automated savings contribute to overall financial well-being.
    Tip: Monitor and adjust automated contributions as your financial situation evolves.

11. **Peace of Mind During Market Volatility:**
    Benefit: Automated investing promotes a disciplined approach, reducing emotional reactions to market fluctuations.
    Tip: Stick to your automated investment plan even during market downturns for long-term benefits.

12. **Adaptability to Life Changes:**
    Benefit: Automated savings can be easily adjusted to accommodate changes in income or expenses.
    Tip: Regularly review and update automated contributions based on life events and financial goals.

By embracing automated savings, you create a systematic and efficient approach to wealth building, enhancing financial stability and setting the stage for long-term prosperity.

Chapter FIVE Investing Fundamentals

Investing is a crucial aspect of wealth building, and understanding the fundamentals is key to making informed decisions. Here are some expert tips and actionable advice to navigate the world of investing:

1. **Risk and Return**
   Explanation: Recognize the relationship between risk and return. Generally, higher returns come with higher risk. Assess your risk tolerance before making investment decisions.

2. **Diversification Strategies**:
3. Explanation: Diversifying your investment portfolio helps spread risk. Invest in a mix of asset classes (stocks, bonds, real estate) to mitigate the impact of poor performance in one area.

4. **Time Horizon**:
   Explanation: Consider your investment time horizon. Longer time horizons allow for a more aggressive approach, while shorter time frames may require a more conservative strategy.

5. **Research and Due Diligence**:
   Explanation: Thoroughly research potential investments. Understand the company's financial health, management, and industry trends before committing your funds.

6. **Costs and Fees:**
7. Explanation: Be aware of investment costs and fees. High fees can significantly impact your returns over time. Choose investments with a reasonable expense ratio.

8. **Stay Informed:**

Explanation: Keep yourself updated on market trends, economic indicators, and global events. Informed decisions are more likely to align with your financial goals.

9. **Long-Term Perspective:**
Explanation: Investing is often most effective with a long-term perspective. Avoid making decisions based on short-term market fluctuations and focus on the overall growth potential.

10. **Emergency Fund First**:
Explanation: Before diving into investments, ensure you have an emergency fund. This provides a financial cushion and prevents the need to sell investments in a downturn to cover unexpected expenses.

11. **Consistent Contributions**:
Explanation: Regularly contribute to your investment accounts. Consistent contributions, even in small amounts, can accumulate over time through the power of compounding.

12. **Rebalance Periodically**:
Explanation: Periodically reassess your portfolio and rebalance if needed. Changes in market conditions or personal financial goals may warrant adjustments to maintain a diversified and aligned investment strategy.

Remember, each individual's financial situation is unique, and it's advisable to consult with a financial advisor to tailor these principles to your specific needs and goals.

Understanding Risks And Return

Investing inherently involves a trade-off between risks and returns. Gaining a solid understanding of this dynamic is crucial for effective wealth building. Here's an exploration of this fundamental concept:

1. **Risk Assessment:**
   Explanation: Before making any investment, assess your risk tolerance.
   This is a personal measure of how much market volatility you can endure without making impulsive decisions.
   It helps align your investments with your comfort level.

2. **Risk Categories:**
   Explanation: Recognize different types of risks, including market risk, inflation risk, and specific investment risks.
   Diversification and proper asset allocation can help manage these risks.

3. **Return Expectations:**
   Explanation: Understand the potential returns associated with different asset classes.
   Generally, riskier investments have the potential for higher returns, but they also come with increased volatility.

4. **Diversification:**
   Explanation: Diversifying your investments across various assets spreads risk.
   While some investments may perform poorly, others may excel, helping to balance overall portfolio performance.

5. **Historical Performance:**
   Explanation: Consider historical performance data when evaluating investments.
   While past performance is not indicative of future results, it can provide insights into how an investment has behaved under different market conditions.

6. **Volatility vs. Stability:**
   Explanation: Volatility is the degree of variation in a trading price series.

Understand that more volatile investments may experience larger price fluctuations, while stable investments may provide more predictable, but typically lower, returns.

7. **Risk-Return Ratio:**
   Explanation: Evaluate the risk-return ratio for each investment.
   This ratio compares the potential return of an investment to the level of risk undertaken. A higher ratio suggests a more favorable balance between risk and reward.

8. **Investment Horizon**:
   Explanation: Consider your investment time horizon.
   Longer-term investments can potentially ride out short-term market fluctuations, allowing for a focus on the overall return potential.

9. **Regular Monitoring:**
   Explanation: Continuously monitor your investments and the market.
   Be prepared to adjust your portfolio if your risk tolerance, financial goals, or market conditions change.

10. **Professional Guidance**:
    Explanation: Seek advice from financial professionals.
    A financial advisor can help you assess your risk tolerance, guide your investment decisions, and create a strategy aligned with your wealth-building goals.

By comprehending the relationship between risks and returns, you empower yourself to make informed investment decisions that align with your financial objectives and risk tolerance.

Diversification Strategies

Diversification is a fundamental strategy in wealth building that involves spreading investments across different asset classes to reduce risk. Here's an exploration of diversification strategies with actionable advice:

1. **Asset Allocation**:
   Explanation: Divide your investment portfolio among different asset classes, such as stocks, bonds, and real estate.
   Each class has a unique risk-return profile, and spreading investments can help manage overall portfolio risk.

2. **Geographic Diversification**:
   Explanation: Invest in assets from different geographical regions.
   Economic conditions can vary globally, and diversifying geographically helps reduce risk associated with regional economic downturns.

3. **Industry Diversification**:
   Explanation: Spread investments across different industries.
   This minimizes the impact of poor performance in a specific sector, as the success of one industry may offset losses in another.

4. **Company Size Diversification**:
   Explanation: Invest in companies of varying sizes. Diversifying between large-cap, mid-cap, and small-cap stocks can provide exposure to different market segments and reduce concentration risk.

5. **Diversification Within Asset Classes**:
   Explanation: Even within a specific asset class, like stocks, diversify further.
   Invest in companies of different sizes, industries, and geographic locations to mitigate risks associated with individual securities.

6. **Balancing Risk and Return**:
   Explanation: Strive for a balanced mix of assets that aligns with your risk tolerance and financial goals.

Avoid overconcentration in high-risk or speculative investments that could jeopardize your overall portfolio.

7. **Regular Portfolio Rebalancing**:
   Explanation: Periodically review and rebalance your portfolio.
   Market fluctuations can alter the original allocation, and rebalancing ensures that your portfolio stays in line with your diversification strategy.

8. **Consider Alternative Investments**:
   Explanation: Explore alternative investments, such as real estate, commodities, or private equity.
   These can provide diversification beyond traditional stocks and bonds, potentially enhancing overall portfolio stability.

9. **Stay Informed About Market Trends**:
   Explanation: Keep abreast of market trends and economic indicators.
   Being aware of changing conditions allows you to adjust your diversification strategy based on evolving market dynamics.

10. **Emergency Fund as a Foundation**:
    Explanation: Before diversifying into various investments, establish a solid emergency fund. This financial cushion ensures you have a safety net and may prevent the need to sell investments in unfavorable market conditions.

By implementing these diversification strategies, you can build a resilient portfolio that is better equipped to withstand market volatility and contribute to long-term wealth building.

Chapter SIX REAL ESTATE INVESTMENT

Real estate investment is a strategy in wealth building that involves acquiring, owning, and managing properties with the expectation of generating income and/or realizing long-term appreciation. Here's a breakdown of key elements and actionable advice for real estate investment:

1. **Types of Real Estate Investments**:
   Explanation: Real estate investments can take various forms, including residential properties (homes, apartments), commercial properties (office buildings, retail spaces), and industrial properties. Each type has its own dynamics and potential returns.

2. **Rental Income**:
   Explanation: One avenue of real estate investment is earning rental income. By leasing out properties, investors can generate a regular stream of cash flow, providing a consistent source of revenue.

3. **Property Appreciation**:
4. Explanation: Real estate has the potential to appreciate over time, leading to an increase in property value. This appreciation can contribute significantly to the overall return on investment when the property is sold.

5. **Leverage through Financing**:
   Explanation: Investors often use financing (mortgages or loans) to acquire real estate, leveraging their capital. This can amplify returns, but it also introduces additional financial risk.

6. **Location Selection**:

Explanation: The location of a property is a critical factor. Choose properties in areas with potential for growth, strong economic fundamentals, and demand for rental properties to enhance investment returns.

7. **Property Management**:
   Explanation: Effective property management is crucial. Whether managed independently or through professional services, maintaining and enhancing the property's value is essential for maximizing returns.

8. **Diversification with Real Estate Investment Trusts (REITs)**:
   Explanation: For diversification without direct property ownership, consider Real Estate Investment Trusts (REITs). These investment vehicles allow you to invest in a portfolio of real estate assets, often traded on the stock market.

9. **Understanding Market Cycles**:
   Explanation: Real estate markets go through cycles of expansion and contraction. Understanding these cycles can help investors make informed decisions about when to buy or sell properties.

10. **Tax Advantages**:
    Explanation: Real estate investments offer various tax advantages, including deductions for mortgage interest, property taxes, and depreciation. Understanding and leveraging these tax benefits can enhance overall returns.

11. **Risk Management**:
    Explanation: Recognize the risks associated with real estate, such as market downturns, property damage, or changes in local regulations. Develop risk mitigation strategies and stay informed about the broader economic landscape.

Real estate investment can be a powerful tool in wealth building, providing both income and potential appreciation. However, success requires careful research, due diligence, and a strategic approach aligned with your financial goals and risk tolerance.

Real estate investment is a dynamic strategy that can significantly contribute to wealth building. Here are expert tips and actionable advice to navigate the complexities of real estate investment:

1. **Define Your Investment Goals**:
   Explanation: Clearly articulate your investment objectives. Whether it's generating rental income, long-term appreciation, or a combination, having well-defined goals will guide your investment decisions.

2. **Conduct Thorough Market Research**:
   Explanation: Research local and national real estate markets. Understand trends, demand-supply dynamics, and economic indicators to identify areas with growth potential and favorable investment conditions.

3. **Budget and Financing**:
   Explanation: Establish a realistic budget and secure financing. Evaluate mortgage options, interest rates, and your ability to meet financial obligations to ensure a sustainable investment.

4. **Location is Key**:
   Explanation: Choose locations strategically. Look for areas with strong job markets, good schools, and amenities that attract potential tenants or buyers. Proximity to public transport and future development plans can also impact property values.

5. **Diversify Your Portfolio**:
   Explanation: Consider diversifying your real estate portfolio. Explore different property types (residential, commercial) and locations to spread risk and optimize returns based on market conditions.

6. **Calculate Return on Investment (ROI):**
    Explanation: Evaluate the potential return on investment for each property. Factor in purchase price, maintenance costs, property management fees, and potential rental income to gauge the profitability of the investment.

7. **Understand Property Management:**
    Explanation: Whether self-managing or hiring a property management service, understand the responsibilities involved. Effective property management ensures tenant satisfaction, property upkeep, and overall investment success.

8. **Stay Informed about Regulations:**
    Explanation: Be aware of local regulations, zoning laws, and landlord-tenant laws. Compliance is crucial to avoid legal issues that could impact your investment returns.

9. **Plan for Market Cycles:**
    Explanation: Realize that real estate markets go through cycles. Timing your investments to align with market conditions can optimize returns. Be prepared to adapt your strategy based on the economic environment.

10. **Build a Network:**
    Explanation: Cultivate relationships with real estate professionals, including real estate agents, contractors, and property managers. A strong network can provide valuable insights, opportunities, and support throughout your investment journey.

11. **Consider Real Estate Investment Trusts (REITs):**
    Explanation: If direct property ownership seems daunting, explore Real Estate Investment Trusts (REITs). They provide a way to invest in real estate without the responsibilities of property management.

12. **Plan for Contingencies:**
    Explanation: Anticipate unexpected challenges. Have a financial buffer for unforeseen expenses, market downturns, or periods of vacancy to ensure your investment remains resilient.

Real estate investment demands a strategic approach and ongoing diligence. By incorporating these expert tips and taking actionable steps, you can navigate the complexities of real estate, enhance your investment success, and contribute to long-term wealth building.

Property Selection Criteria

Investing in real estate is a powerful wealth-building strategy, but success hinges on the art of property selection. In "Wealth Building 101," we unravel the key criteria to guide your property investment decisions, ensuring a solid foundation for financial growth.

1. **Location, Location, Location:**
   Explanation: The importance of location cannot be overstated. Choose properties in areas with potential for growth, considering factors like proximity to amenities, schools, transportation, and economic development.

2. **Market Trends and Analysis**:
   Explanation: Stay ahead of market trends by conducting thorough research. Analyze past and present market data, assess property values, and anticipate future trends. This knowledge will empower you to make informed investment decisions.

3. **Rental Income Potential:**
   Explanation: A property's ability to generate rental income is a crucial aspect of wealth building. Evaluate the rental market in the area, demand for housing, and potential rental yields to ensure a steady income stream.

4. **Property Condition and Maintenance**:
   Explanation: Assess the current condition of the property and estimate potential maintenance costs. A well-maintained property not only attracts better tenants but also minimizes unforeseen expenses, safeguarding your long-term investment.

5. **Future Development Plans**:
   Explanation: Investigate municipal plans and development projects in the area. A growing community often translates to increased property values. Being aware of future developments allows you to position your investment strategically.

6. **Affordability and Financing:**
    Explanation: Ensure the property aligns with your financial capacity. Evaluate financing options, interest rates, and potential returns. A property that fits within your budget and offers favorable financing terms contributes to a sustainable investment.

7. **Potential for Appreciation:**
    Explanation: Look beyond the present value and consider the property's potential for appreciation. Factors such as neighborhood improvement, infrastructure development, and economic growth contribute to long-term value appreciation.

8. **Diversification Strategy:**
    Explanation: Diversify your property portfolio to spread risk. Consider different types of properties (e.g., residential, commercial) and locations. This strategy helps mitigate risks associated with market fluctuations in specific sectors.

9. **Legal and Regulatory Compliance:**
    Explanation: Ensure the property complies with local regulations and zoning laws. Understanding legal aspects prevents potential complications and ensures a smooth, lawful investment process.

10. **Exit Strategy:**
    Explanation: Develop a clear exit strategy before investing. Whether it's selling for profit, leveraging equity, or passing it on to heirs, having a well-defined plan aligns your investment with long-term financial goals.

By integrating these property selection criteria into your wealth-building journey, "Wealth Building 101" empowers you to make sound real estate investment decisions. Navigate the dynamic world of property investment with confidence, ensuring each investment propels you closer to financial prosperity.

Finance Option

In the context of "Wealth Building 101," finance options refer to the diverse strategies and tools available for individuals to fund their investment ventures, manage their money wisely, and optimize their financial growth. These options are designed to provide flexibility, mitigate risks, and align with specific wealth-building goals. Here's a breakdown of key finance options explored in the book:

1. **Savings and Budgeting:**
   Explanation: "Wealth Building 101" emphasizes the fundamental practice of saving and budgeting. Establishing a disciplined savings routine and creating a realistic budget are foundational steps for individuals looking to accumulate wealth.

2. **Investment Portfolios:**
   Explanation: Diversifying investments across various asset classes, such as stocks, bonds, and real estate, is a core finance option. The book delves into crafting strategic investment portfolios that balance risk and reward, fostering long-term financial growth.

3. **Strategic Debt Management:**
   Explanation: While debt is often viewed negatively, "Wealth Building 101" explores how strategic debt management can be a powerful tool. Leveraging debt for investments that yield higher returns, such as real estate or entrepreneurial ventures, is discussed to optimize financial outcomes.

4. **Retirement Accounts:**
   Explanation: The book covers the importance of utilizing retirement accounts, such as 401(k)s or IRAs, as effective finance options. Understanding how to maximize

contributions, choose appropriate investments, and leverage tax advantages is crucial for building wealth over time.

5. **Emergency Funds and Liquidity**:
Explanation: "Wealth Building 101" stresses the significance of maintaining emergency funds for unforeseen circumstances. The book provides insights into creating liquidity strategies, ensuring individuals can navigate financial challenges without jeopardizing their long-term goals.

6. **Passive Income Streams**:
Explanation: Exploring avenues for passive income is a key finance option highlighted in the book. From real estate investments to dividend-paying stocks, the focus is on creating sustainable income streams that contribute to overall financial health.

7. **Entrepreneurial Ventures:**
Explanation: For those inclined towards entrepreneurship, the book delves into finance options for starting and scaling businesses. This includes understanding funding sources, managing cash flow, and optimizing financial strategies for entrepreneurial success.

8. **Tax-Efficient Strategies**:
Explanation: "Wealth Building 101" educates readers on tax-efficient finance options, ensuring individuals can minimize tax liabilities and maximize returns. Strategies like tax-advantaged accounts and smart tax planning are explored to enhance overall financial efficiency.

9. **Insurance and Risk Management**:Explanation: Mitigating financial risks through insurance is a crucial aspect covered in the book. Understanding how different insurance products align with wealth-building goals and protect against unforeseen events is emphasized.

10. **Estate Planning**:
Explanation: Finance options extend to estate planning, ensuring that individuals can pass on their wealth efficiently to future generations. The book explores strategies for minimizing estate taxes and establishing a legacy that endures.

"Wealth Building 101" provides a comprehensive guide to navigating these finance options, empowering readers to make informed decisions that align with their unique financial aspirations. By understanding and leveraging these tools, individuals can pave the way for sustained financial success and prosperity.

Chapter SEVEN Retirement Planning

Retirement planning, a cornerstone of financial well-being, takes center stage in "Wealth Building 101." This section of the book provides expert insights and practical advice to empower individuals in securing a comfortable and fulfilling retirement. Here's an overview and explanation of retirement planning as presented in the book:

1. **Setting Clear Retirement Goals**:
    Explanation: "Wealth Building 101" begins by emphasizing the importance of setting clear and realistic retirement goals. Understanding the lifestyle one envisions during retirement is the foundation for creating a strategic financial plan.

2. **Early Start and Compound Growth**:
    Explanation: The book underscores the advantage of an early start to retirement planning. By harnessing the power of compound growth, individuals can maximize the growth potential of their retirement savings over time.

3. **Diversification of Retirement Assets**:
    Explanation: Diversifying retirement assets is a key strategy explored in the book. Balancing investments across various vehicles, such as 401(k)s, IRAs, and other tax-advantaged accounts, helps manage risk and optimize returns.

4. **Income Replacement Strategies**:
Explanation: "Wealth Building 101" delves into effective income replacement strategies. Understanding how to replace a significant portion of pre-retirement income ensures a smooth transition to retirement living without compromising one's standard of living.

5. **Social Security Optimization**:
Explanation: The book provides insights into optimizing Social Security benefits. Understanding when and how to claim Social Security can significantly impact the total income received during retirement, and the book navigates readers through these critical decisions.

6. **Healthcare and Long-Term Care Planning**:
Explanation: Addressing healthcare costs and long-term care is a vital aspect of retirement planning. "Wealth Building 101" explores strategies for securing adequate healthcare coverage and preparing for potential long-term care expenses.

7. **Budgeting for Retirement**:
Explanation: The book emphasizes the importance of realistic budgeting for retirement. Readers gain insights into crafting a budget that aligns with their retirement goals, ensuring financial stability throughout their post-career years.

8. **Downsizing and Lifestyle Adjustments**:
Explanation: "Wealth Building 101" acknowledges the potential need for downsizing and lifestyle adjustments during retirement. Understanding how these decisions can impact finances is crucial for maintaining a comfortable and sustainable retirement.

9. **Estate Planning for Retirement Assets**:
Explanation: The book delves into estate planning considerations for retirement assets. Readers gain insights into minimizing estate taxes, designating beneficiaries, and ensuring a smooth transfer of wealth to heirs.

10. **Adapting Retirement Plans**:
   Explanation: Recognizing that life is dynamic, the book encourages readers to adapt
   their retirement plans as circumstances change. This includes reassessing goals,
   adjusting investment strategies, and ensuring ongoing financial resilience.

"Wealth Building 101" positions retirement planning as a dynamic and integral part of the
wealth-building journey. By providing expert tips and actionable advice in each of these areas,
the book equips individuals to navigate the complexities of retirement planning with confidence,
ensuring a secure and fulfilling post-career life.

Importance Of Early Planning

In "Wealth Building 101," the emphasis on early planning is a fundamental principle that underpins the entire wealth-building journey. Here's a breakdown of the importance of early planning as explored in the book:

1. **Compound Growth Advantage:**
   Explanation: "Wealth Building 101" stresses the significant advantage of compound growth, where earnings on an investment, both capital gains and interest, earn interest over time. Early planning allows individuals to harness the full power of compounding, maximizing the growth potential of their investments.

2. **Extended Time Horizon:**
   Explanation: The book underscores the extended time horizon available to early planners. Starting early provides a longer runway to weather market fluctuations, take calculated risks, and recover from any setbacks, ultimately contributing to a more resilient and successful wealth-building strategy.

3. **Increased Risk Tolerance:**
   Explanation: Early planners have the luxury of a higher risk tolerance. They can afford to invest in potentially higher-yielding but riskier assets, knowing that there is ample time to recover from any short-term losses. This proactive approach can lead to greater returns in the long run.

4. **Financial Education and Skill Development:**
   Explanation: Beginning the wealth-building journey early allows individuals to invest time in financial education and skill development. Early planners can learn from experiences, refine their investment strategies, and build a solid foundation of knowledge to make informed decisions throughout their financial journey.

5. **Long-Term Goal Clarity**:
Explanation: Early planning enables individuals to establish clear long-term financial goals. Whether it's buying a home, funding education, or retiring comfortably, having well-defined goals from the outset allows for more strategic and purposeful wealth-building efforts.

6. **Flexible Lifestyle Choices**:Explanation: Those who start planning early have greater flexibility in making lifestyle choices. Whether it's pursuing entrepreneurial ventures, taking career risks, or exploring diverse investment opportunities, early planners have the freedom to shape their financial journey with more agility.

7. **Emergency Fund Accumulation**:
Explanation: Early planners can prioritize building robust emergency funds. Having a financial safety net in place early on provides a buffer against unexpected expenses or economic downturns, reducing the risk of derailing long-term wealth-building goals.

8. **Debt Management and Reduction**:Explanation: Early planning allows individuals to strategically manage and reduce debt. Addressing debts early in the wealth-building journey ensures that more financial resources can be directed towards investments and savings, accelerating overall wealth accumulation.

9. **Establishing Good Financial Habits:**
Explanation: The book encourages the development of good financial habits from an early stage. These habits, such as disciplined saving, budgeting, and strategic investing, become ingrained over time, setting the stage for consistent and sustainable wealth-building practices.

10. **Psychological Well-Being:**
Explanation: Early planners often experience reduced financial stress and enhanced psychological well-being. Knowing that a comprehensive plan is in place provides a

sense of security and confidence, allowing individuals to focus on achieving their goals without the burden of financial uncertainty.In essence,

"Wealth Building 101" makes a compelling case for early planning as a linchpin for success. By starting the wealth-building journey early, individuals position themselves to capitalize on unique advantages, navigate challenges more effectively, and ultimately achieve enduring financial prosperity.

Retirement Account Option

In "Wealth Building 101," the exploration of retirement account options is a cornerstone of the book's guidance on securing financial well-being during retirement. Let's delve into the various retirement account options and the actionable advice provided in the book:

1. **401(k) Plans:**
    Explanation: Employer-sponsored 401(k) plans are highlighted, allowing employees to contribute pre-tax income. "Wealth Building 101" advises readers on optimizing contributions, taking advantage of employer matches, and navigating investment choices within these plans.

2. **Individual Retirement Accounts (IRAs):**
    Explanation: Traditional and Roth IRAs take center stage, offering distinct tax advantages. The book provides actionable advice on choosing between the two based on individual circumstances, as well as guidance on contribution limits and investment strategies.

3. **SEP IRA (Simplified Employee Pension IRA):**
    Explanation: For self-employed individuals and small business owners, the book introduces SEP IRAs. Actionable advice covers contribution limits, eligibility criteria, and leveraging the flexibility of SEP IRAs for retirement savings.

4. **SIMPLE IRA (Savings Incentive Match Plan for Employees):**
    Explanation: The book addresses SIMPLE IRAs, emphasizing their suitability for small businesses. Readers receive actionable insights on maximizing benefits through

employer and employee contributions and navigating the simplicity of these retirement plans.

5. **Solo 401(k):**
   Explanation: Tailored for self-employed individuals, the Solo 401(k) is explored as a versatile option. "Wealth Building 101" offers practical advice on contribution limits, considerations for business owners, and strategies to optimize retirement savings through Solo 401(k)s.

6. **403(b) Plans:**
   Explanation: Geared towards employees in nonprofit organizations and public schools, 403(b) plans are discussed. The book provides actionable advice on understanding contribution limits, investment options, and the unique features of these retirement accounts.

7. **457(b) Plans:Explanation:** The book touches on 457(b) plans, commonly available to government employees. Actionable advice includes insights into contribution limits, potential benefits, and the role these plans play in government employees' retirement planning.

8. **Government Thrift Savings Plan (TSP):**
   Explanation: TSP, designed for federal employees and uniformed services members, is explored. Practical advice in "Wealth Building 101" covers contribution options, investment funds, and the strategic role TSP plays in federal employees' retirement planning.

9. **Health Savings Account (HSA):**
   Explanation: The intersection of healthcare and retirement planning is addressed through HSAs. The book provides actionable advice on utilizing HSAs for both medical expenses and long-term retirement savings, leveraging their unique tax advantages.

10. In-Service Withdrawals and Rollovers:
   Explanation: Recognizing the fluidity of career paths, the book offers insights into
   in-service withdrawals and rollovers. Actionable advice guides readers on transferring
   funds between retirement accounts during their working years, optimizing flexibility and
   investment choices.

In essence, "Wealth Building 101" serves as a practical guide, not only introducing various
retirement account options but also providing actionable advice to help readers make informed
decisions aligned with their financial goals. The book empowers individuals to navigate the
complexities of retirement planning with confidence and effectiveness.

Chapter EIGHT Debt Management

Debt management is a crucial aspect of financial success, and in "Wealth Building 101," it is explored as a strategic component of the broader wealth-building journey. Here's an overview and explanation of debt management as presented in the book:

1. **Debt Assessment and Organization:**
   Explanation: The book begins by advising readers to assess their existing debts. This involves organizing and categorizing debts, understanding interest rates, and creating a comprehensive overview of the current financial landscape.

2. **Prioritizing High-Interest Debts:**
   Explanation: "Wealth Building 101" provides actionable advice on prioritizing high-interest debts. By tackling debts with the highest interest rates first, individuals can minimize the overall interest paid over time, accelerating their journey to debt freedom.

3. **Creating a Realistic Budget:**
   Explanation: Practical budgeting strategies are explored to assist readers in managing their finances effectively. The book emphasizes the importance of creating a realistic budget that allocates funds for debt repayment while meeting essential living expenses.

4. **Emergency Fund Establishment:**
   Explanation: The book highlights the role of an emergency fund in debt management. Actionable advice includes guidance on building a financial safety net to cover unexpected expenses, reducing the reliance on credit for emergencies.

5. **Negotiating Interest Rates**:
   Explanation: Negotiating lower interest rates on existing debts is presented as a proactive strategy. "Wealth Building 101" provides actionable tips on approaching creditors to explore opportunities for reduced interest rates, potentially lightening the burden of debt.

6. **Debt Consolidation Considerations:**
   Explanation: The book explores the option of debt consolidation and offers actionable advice on when and how to consolidate debts. It provides insights into the potential benefits and risks associated with consolidation strategies.

7. **Snowball vs. Avalanche Method:**
   Explanation: Readers are introduced to two popular debt repayment methods: the snowball method and the avalanche method. Actionable advice is provided on choosing the approach that aligns with individual preferences and motivations, optimizing the debt repayment process.

8. **Financial Counseling and Professional Assistance:**
   Explanation: Recognizing that some individuals may benefit from professional guidance, "Wealth Building 101" offers actionable advice on seeking financial counseling. This can involve working with experts to create personalized debt management plans and strategies.

9. **Avoiding Accumulation of New Debt:**
   Explanation: The book underscores the importance of breaking the cycle of debt accumulation. Actionable advice includes cultivating habits that prevent the incurrence of new debts, fostering long-term financial health.

10. **Celebrating Milestones and Progress:**
    Explanation: To maintain motivation, the book advises readers to celebrate milestones in debt repayment. Acknowledging progress, no matter how small, can reinforce positive financial habits and fuel the momentum toward becoming debt-free.

"Wealth Building 101" positions debt management as a proactive and empowering step in the wealth-building journey. By providing actionable advice on assessing, prioritizing, and strategically repaying debts, the book equips readers with the tools to achieve financial freedom and build a solid foundation for lasting prosperity.

.Tackling High Interest- debt

In "Wealth Building 101," addressing high-interest debt is a pivotal aspect of the comprehensive strategy for financial success. The book provides actionable advice to empower individuals in tackling high-interest debts effectively. Here's an overview and explanation:

1. **Interest Rate Assessment:**
   Explanation: The book begins by advising readers to assess the interest rates on their debts. This involves creating a list of debts along with their corresponding interest rates, providing a clear understanding of which debts are the most costly over time.

2. **Prioritizing High-Interest Debts**:
   Explanation: "Wealth Building 101" emphasizes the urgency of prioritizing high-interest debts. Readers are provided with actionable advice on creating a repayment plan that targets debts with the highest interest rates first, minimizing the overall interest burden.

3. **Minimum Payments vs. Extra Payments:**
   Explanation: Practical guidance is offered on the balance between making minimum payments and allocating extra funds toward high-interest debts. The book encourages readers to pay more than the minimum when possible, accelerating the repayment process and reducing interest accrued.

4. **Debt Snowball Method:**
   Explanation: "Wealth Building 101" introduces the debt snowball method as an actionable strategy. This involves focusing on paying off the smallest debts first, gaining psychological wins and momentum that can be redirected toward larger high-interest debts.

5. **Debt Avalanche Method**:
   Explanation: The book explores the debt avalanche method as an alternative strategy. This method involves prioritizing debts with the highest interest rates regardless of their size. Actionable advice is provided on implementing the avalanche method for efficient interest reduction.

6. **Negotiating Lower Interest Rates**:
   Explanation: Recognizing the potential impact of interest rates on debt repayment, the book offers actionable advice on negotiating lower rates. Readers learn strategies for approaching creditors to discuss and potentially lower interest rates, easing the overall burden.

7. **Transferring Balances Strategically**:
   Explanation: For individuals with multiple high-interest debts, the book provides insights into strategic balance transfers. Actionable advice covers considerations for consolidating debts onto lower-interest accounts, optimizing repayment terms.

8. **Creating a Repayment Plan**:
   Explanation: "Wealth Building 101" guides readers in creating a detailed repayment plan. This includes setting realistic goals, allocating funds strategically, and maintaining consistency in debt repayment efforts.

9. **Identifying and Addressing Root Causes**:
   Explanation: The book encourages readers to identify and address the root causes of high-interest debt accumulation. Actionable advice involves examining spending habits, creating budgets, and cultivating financial habits that prevent future debt challenges.

10. **Seeking Professional Guidance:**
    Explanation: Recognizing that tackling high-interest debt can be complex, the book advises seeking professional guidance when needed. Actionable steps include

considering financial counseling or consulting with debt management professionals to create personalized plans.

By combining these actionable strategies, "Wealth Building 101" equips individuals with the tools to effectively tackle high-interest debt. The book not only addresses the immediate financial challenge but also fosters habits and approaches that contribute to sustained financial health and wealth-building success.

Credit Score Improvement

Improving your credit score is a vital component of a solid financial foundation, and "Wealth Building 101" provides expert tips and actionable advice for this purpose. Here's an overview and explanation of credit score improvement as presented in the book:

1. **Credit Report Review:**
   Explanation: The book advises readers to start by obtaining and reviewing their credit reports. Understanding the information on these reports is crucial for identifying errors, inaccuracies, or areas that need improvement.

2. **Check Credit Score Regularly**:
   Explanation: Regular monitoring of your credit score is emphasized in "Wealth Building 101." Actionable advice includes using reputable credit monitoring services to stay informed about changes in your score and factors affecting it.

3. **Addressing Errors and Disputes**:
   Explanation: The book provides actionable steps for addressing errors or discrepancies on your credit report. This involves submitting disputes to credit bureaus to rectify inaccuracies that may be negatively impacting your score.

4. **Paying Bills on Time**:
   Explanation: Timely payment of bills is a fundamental strategy for credit score improvement. "Wealth Building 101" offers actionable advice on setting up reminders, automating payments, and establishing a routine to ensure bills are paid promptly.

5. **Reducing Credit Card Balances**:
   Explanation: The book explores the impact of credit card balances on your credit score. Actionable advice includes strategies for reducing credit card balances, paying off high-interest debts, and managing credit utilization to improve your score.

6. **Strategic Use of Credit**:
   Explanation: "Wealth Building 101" provides insights into the strategic use of credit. Actionable advice involves responsibly managing credit accounts, diversifying types of credit, and avoiding unnecessary or impulse credit applications.

7. **Negotiating with Creditors**:
   Explanation: The book suggests negotiating with creditors as an actionable strategy. Readers learn how to communicate with creditors to explore options such as lower interest rates, debt settlement, or revised payment plans to positively impact their credit.

8. **Building a Positive Credit History**:Explanation: The importance of building a positive credit history is highlighted. Actionable advice in the book includes keeping older accounts open, responsibly managing credit over time, and avoiding actions that may negatively impact your credit history.

9. **Avoiding Collections and Charge-Offs**:
   Explanation: The book provides actionable advice on avoiding collections and charge-offs. Strategies involve negotiating with creditors, setting up payment plans, and addressing outstanding debts to prevent negative entries on your credit report.

10. **Patience and Consistency**:
    Explanation: "Wealth Building 101" underscores the importance of patience and consistency in credit score improvement. Actionable advice includes recognizing that improvements take time and maintaining positive credit habits consistently over the long term.

By implementing these actionable strategies, individuals can not only repair damaged credit but also build a strong credit foundation for future financial endeavors. "Wealth Building 101" serves as a comprehensive guide, offering practical steps to empower readers in their journey towards a healthier credit profile and overall financial success.

Chapter NINE Conclusion

In the concluding chapters of "Wealth Building 101," readers find a synthesis of expert insights and practical guidance, solidifying the principles and strategies outlined throughout the book. The conclusion serves as a roadmap for individuals navigating their wealth-building journey, summarizing key takeaways and encouraging a proactive approach toward financial success.

1. **Recap of Key Principles**:

    Explanation: The conclusion begins with a recap of the fundamental principles presented in the book. It revisits the importance of early planning, diversified investments, debt management, and strategic use of financial tools.

2. **Empowerment Through Knowledge**:

    Explanation: "Wealth Building 101" emphasizes the role of knowledge in financial empowerment. The conclusion highlights how understanding various aspects of personal finance, from investments to debt management, equips individuals to make informed decisions and take control of their financial future.

3. **Long-Term Perspective**:

    Explanation: Encouraging a long-term perspective, the conclusion emphasizes that building wealth is a journey rather than a destination. Readers are reminded that consistent and strategic actions over time lead to enduring financial success.

4. **Adaptability and Resilience**:

Explanation: Acknowledging the dynamic nature of financial landscapes, the conclusion stresses the importance of adaptability and resilience. Wealth Building 101 encourages readers to adjust strategies as needed, staying resilient in the face of economic changes and personal circumstances.

5. **Holistic Approach to Wealth**:
   Explanation: The book concludes by reinforcing the idea that wealth is not solely measured in monetary terms. It encompasses financial stability, a comfortable retirement, and the ability to pursue meaningful goals. A holistic approach to wealth includes physical, mental, and emotional well-being.

6. **Actionable Steps for Readers**:
   Explanation: To empower readers to take immediate action, the conclusion provides a concise list of actionable steps. Whether it's setting financial goals, diversifying investments, or managing debt, these steps serve as a practical guide for applying the book's principles.

7. **Continued Learning and Growth**:
   Explanation: The conclusion encourages a commitment to continued learning and personal growth. Wealth Building 101 positions itself as a starting point, and readers are urged to explore further, stay informed about financial trends, and adapt their strategies as they progress on their wealth-building journey.

8. **Celebrating Achievements**:
   Explanation: Celebrating financial milestones is emphasized as a crucial aspect of the conclusion. Whether it's paying off debts, reaching investment goals, or achieving a higher credit score, acknowledging and celebrating achievements helps maintain motivation and momentum.

9. **Community and Support:**Explanation: Recognizing that wealth-building journeys can benefit from community and support, the conclusion encourages readers to share their experiences, seek advice, and build connections with like-minded individuals. A supportive network can provide encouragement and valuable insights.

10. **A Call to Action**:
>Explanation: The conclusion concludes with a call to action. Readers are invited to take charge of their financial destiny, armed with the knowledge and practical strategies provided in "Wealth Building 101." The call to action encourages readers to embrace their financial potential and embark on a path to lasting prosperity.

In essence, the conclusion of "Wealth Building 101" leaves readers inspired, informed, and equipped with the tools to navigate the complexities of personal finance. It serves as a motivational closing chapter, encouraging individuals to implement the expert tips and actionable advice, ultimately propelling them towards a future of financial success and well-being.

Rcaps Of Key Wealth Building principles

As we recap the key wealth-building principles from "Wealth Building 101," we revisit the foundational concepts that form the backbone of the expert insights and actionable advice provided in the book. These principles serve as a compass for individuals navigating their financial journey:

Early Planning and Compound Growth:
Explanation: "Wealth Building 101" underscores the significance of early planning. Starting early allows individuals to harness the power of compound growth, maximizing the potential returns on investments over time.

Diversified Investments:
Explanation: Diversification is a cornerstone principle. The book advocates for spreading investments across various asset classes to manage risk effectively. A well-diversified portfolio helps individuals weather market fluctuations and optimize long-term gains.

Strategic Debt Management:
Explanation: The importance of strategic debt management is highlighted. The book guides readers on understanding and addressing debts, leveraging them strategically for investments, and minimizing overall financial liabilities.Emergency Funds and Liquidity:Explanation: Maintaining emergency funds is a crucial principle. Having a financial safety net provides resilience in the face of unforeseen circumstances, ensuring individuals can navigate challenges without compromising long-term financial goals.

Passive Income Streams:
Explanation: "Wealth Building 101" promotes the creation of passive income streams. From real estate investments to dividend-paying stocks, passive income adds a layer of financial security and accelerates wealth accumulation.

Entrepreneurial Ventures:
Explanation: For those inclined towards entrepreneurship, the book explores the principles of starting and scaling businesses. It covers funding strategies, cash flow management, and financial optimization for entrepreneurial success.

Tax-Efficient Strategies:
Explanation: The book educates readers on tax-efficient wealth-building strategies. This includes utilizing tax-advantaged accounts, smart tax planning, and understanding how to minimize tax liabilities while maximizing returns.

Insurance and Risk Management:
Explanation: Mitigating financial risks through insurance is a crucial principle. The book explores different insurance products and how they align with wealth-building goals, providing a comprehensive approach to risk management.

Estate Planning:
Explanation: Wealth preservation is addressed through estate planning. Readers learn about minimizing estate taxes, designating beneficiaries, and ensuring a smooth transfer of wealth to future generations.

Retirement Planning:
Explanation: The book emphasizes the importance of retirement planning. Readers gain insights into setting clear retirement goals, maximizing contributions to retirement accounts, and navigating income replacement strategies for a comfortable post-career life.

These key wealth-building principles collectively form a comprehensive framework for financial success. "Wealth Building 101" positions them as actionable guidelines, empowering readers to make informed decisions, adapt to changing circumstances, and cultivate enduring financial prosperity.

Encouragement For Long Term Success

In "Wealth Building 101," the encouragement for long-term success serves as a motivational cornerstone to inspire individuals on their financial journey. The book provides expert tips and actionable advice to instill a mindset that fosters enduring prosperity:**

1. **Patience as a Virtue:**Explanation: The book emphasizes that wealth-building is a marathon, not a sprint. Encouragement is provided around the virtue of patience, reminding readers that sustainable success takes time. Consistent, strategic actions compound over the long term, yielding significant results.**

2. **Resilience in the Face of Challenges:**Explanation: Encouragement is given to cultivate resilience when facing financial challenges. The book acknowledges that setbacks are a natural part of any journey but emphasizes that overcoming obstacles contributes to personal and financial growth.**

3. **Adaptability to Changing Circumstances:**Explanation: Wealth Building 101 encourages readers to embrace adaptability. Financial landscapes evolve, and being open to adjusting strategies based on changing circumstances is a key principle for long-term success.

4. **Learning from Setbacks:**Explanation: Instead of viewing setbacks as failures, the book encourages readers to see them as learning opportunities. Every challenge presents a chance to refine strategies, enhance financial literacy, and build resilience for future endeavors.

5. **Consistency in Financial Habits**:Explanation: Encouragement is provided for maintaining consistent financial habits. The book stresses that daily, disciplined actions, whether it's saving, investing, or budgeting, contribute significantly to long-term financial success.
6. **Celebrating Milestones, Big and Small:**
Explanation: Recognizing and celebrating milestones along the way is encouraged. Whether paying off a debt, reaching a savings goal, or achieving a favorable credit score, celebrating these achievements reinforces positive financial habits and provides motivation for the journey ahead.

7. **Staying Informed and Continuously Learning**:Explanation: Encouragement is given for a commitment to continuous learning. Staying informed about financial trends, investment strategies, and personal finance best practices empowers individuals to make informed decisions for long-term success.

8. **Building a Supportive Financial Community**:Explanation: The book encourages readers to build a supportive financial community. Sharing experiences, seeking advice, and connecting with like-minded individuals provide a valuable support system that enhances motivation and accountability.

9. **Mindful Spending and Lifestyle Choices**:Explanation: Wealth Building 101 promotes encouragement for mindful spending and lifestyle choices. Being intentional about expenditures ensures resources are directed toward long-term financial goals, contributing to sustained success.

10. **Vision and Purpose in Wealth Building**:Explanation: Encouragement is provided to connect wealth-building efforts with a clear vision and purpose. Understanding the why behind financial goals instills a sense of purpose, making the journey more meaningful and motivating for the long term.

In summary, the encouragement for long-term success in "Wealth Building 101" goes beyond financial strategies; it nurtures a mindset that fosters resilience, adaptability, and a commitment to continuous improvement. By embracing these principles, individuals are empowered not only to achieve financial success but to sustain it over the course of their lives.

As we reach the final conclusion of "Expert Tips and Actionable Advice," this journey through the realms of personal finance concludes with a synthesis of knowledge, motivation, and practical strategies. The book serves as a compass for individuals navigating the intricacies of wealth building, offering insights that extend beyond mere financial transactions.

In closing, "Expert Tips and Actionable Advice" is not merely a guidebook but a companion for individuals striving for financial well-being. It provides the tools to navigate the complex landscape of personal finance, empowering readers to shape their financial destinies. As this book concludes, it leaves a lasting message: financial success is not just about the numbers; it's about creating a life of purpose, resilience, and enduring prosperity. May this journey be transformative and may your financial goals be not just achieved but surpassed.

www.ingramcontent.com/pod-product-compliance
Lightning Source LLC
Chambersburg PA
CBHW071100260726
48661CB00006B/2362